Rain Forest

Written by Cindy Barden
Illustrated by Nancee McClure

A rain forest is like

a wild garden zoo

filled with strange plants

and animals, too.

Many animals live

on the dark forest floor

like beetles, dragonflies,

ogs, and more.

Air plants and vine

ling to the trees.

The tops of the tree

orm the canopy.

During the day

14

oisy birds take flight.

**But the rain forest is full
of hunters at night.**